*"If we know what to do,
then why aren't we doing it?"*

Evidence-Based Practice IMPLEMENTATION

Nurse leader's guide to successful EBP implementation

By

Shirley Ellen Bomhoff

MSN, Lean Six Sigma Black Belt

With gratitude to W. Edwards Deming,

my children's great grandfather,

who inspired me to pursue a professional career in

process and systems improvement,

supporting healthcare organizations in the

relentless pursuit of quality outcomes for patients,

families, and associates.

In honor of my sons,
Conor Deming Cahill

Colin Edwards Cahill,

who continually inspire me with their tenacity for life,

their humor, and love of family

Why is it so challenging to implement evidence-based practice successfully?

There is wide agreement that the implementation of evidence-based practice (EBP) leads to a higher quality of care and better patient outcomes. However, by all accounts, nurses encounter many barriers when implementing EBP. [4] In my three decades of practice in performance improvement (PI), I posit that education and mentoring alone are insufficient to successfully implement EBP.

It is important to approach this challenge with curiosity and compassion. There are many true barriers encountered by bedside nurses and clinicians that need to be surfaced, understood, and either mitigated or eliminated.

As formal and informal leaders, it is our responsibility to design and continually improve the clinical processes we expect caregivers to perform. The processes and guidelines should make it easy for associates to do the right thing every time.

What is evidence-based practice, and why is it relevant?

The classic definition of evidence-based practice (EBP) is from Dr. David Sackett.

> EBP is *"the conscientious, explicit, and judicious use of current best evidence in making decisions about the care of the individual patient. It means integrating individual clinical expertise with the best available external clinical evidence from systematic research".*[1]

EBP has developed over time to integrate the best research evidence, clinical expertise, the patient's individual values and circumstances, and the characteristics of the practice in which the health professional works. [2] (see Figure 1)

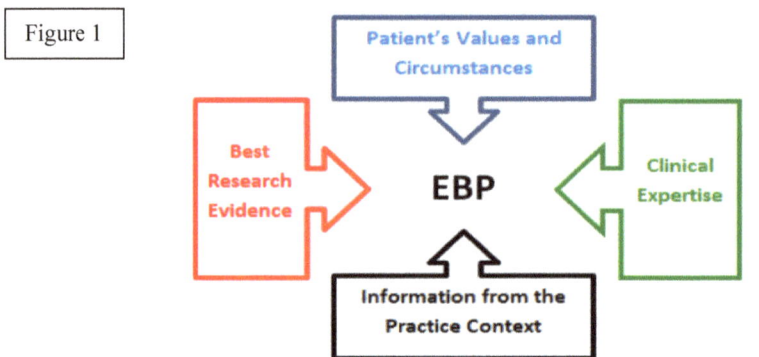

Figure 1

Evidence-Based Practice involves clinical reasoning to integrate information from four sources

One of the roles of the Nursing Professional Development (NPD) practitioner in the 2022 edition of the Nursing Scope and Standards of Practice is a champion for scientific inquiry. In this role, the NPD practitioner promotes a spirit of inquiry, the generation and dissemination of new knowledge, and the use of evidence to advance NPD practice, guide clinical practice, and improve the quality of care for the patient. Scholarly inquiry is a standard of practice within that role. [2]

NPD practitioners, along with senior nursing leaders, nurse educators, quality managers, and frontline nursing leaders, both formal and informal, can utilize this guide to achieve successful adoption of EBP. Several examples in this guide are presented in the context of a strategic organizational goal to reduce central line associated bloodstream infections.

What are the most frequently used EBP Models?

The four most frequently used EBP models and their primary focus are [2]:

1. **Iowa Model**:

    o Focus is on implementing evidence-based practice changes

2. **Advancing Research and Clinical Practice through Close Collaboration (ARCC) Model**:

- Focus is on advancing EBP in systems by using EBP mentors and control and cognitive behavioral therapies.

3. **Star Model of Knowledge Transformation:**

    - Focus is on providing a framework for approaching EBP.

4. **John Hopkins Nursing Evidence-based Practice (JHNEBP) Model:**

    - Focus is on a problem-based approach to clinical decision-making accompanied by tools to guide its use.

Of the most well-known EBP models, the Iowa EBP Model attempts to address the pilot and implementation phases most clearly. [4] However, I believe the model applies a broad-brush approach to the most critical steps necessary for successful implementation. This guide expands upon the Iowa EBP Model, providing detailed novel approaches utilizing proven performance improvement techniques, tools, and strategies.

The Iowa model (see Figure 2) was revised and updated in 2017 by the Iowa Model Collaborative. Changes in the healthcare environment, such as a focus on implementation science and emphasis on patient engagement, prompted a reevaluation, revision, and validation of the model. This model differs from other frameworks by linking practice changes within the system. [3]

Model changes included an expansion of piloting, implementation, patient engagement, and sustaining change. The piloting and implementation steps are critical to success and will be described in detail. If performed without rigor, these steps become the failure mode and lead to resistance and a high degree of unwarranted variation.

Figure 2 — Iowa Model Process Map

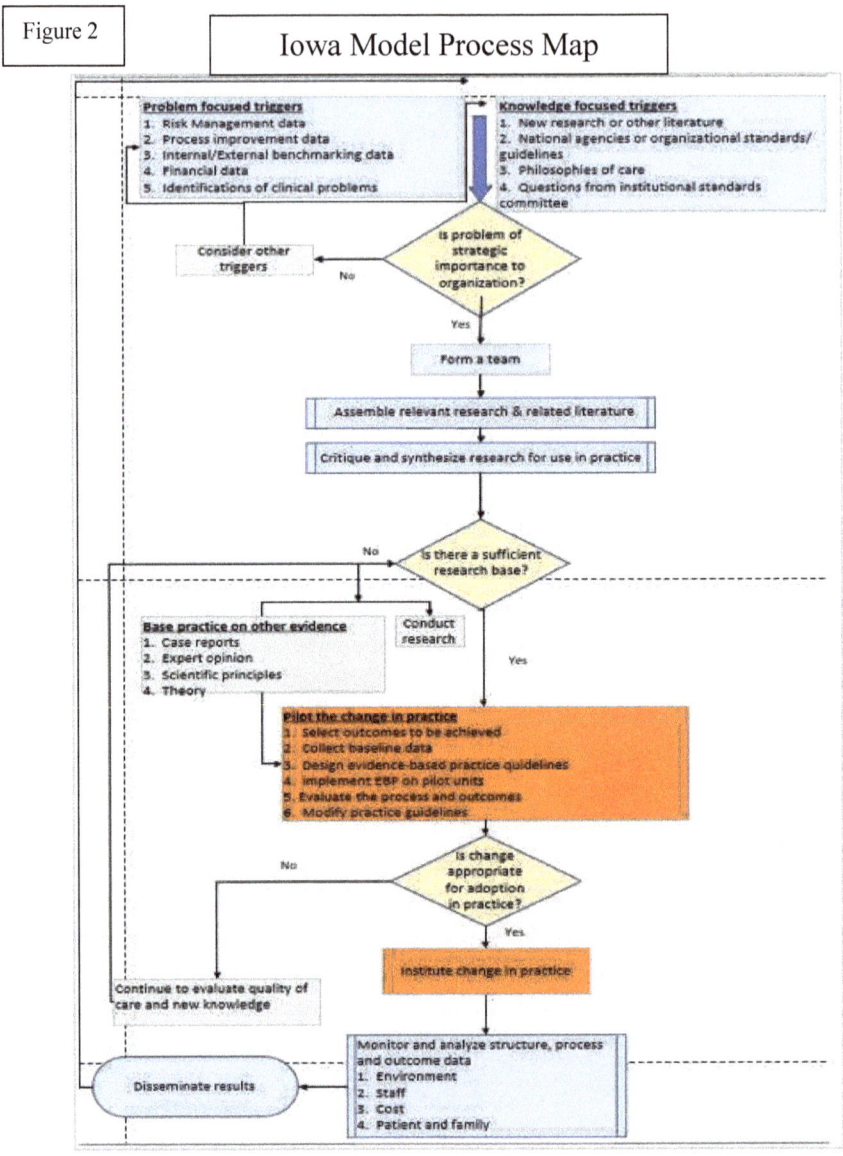

This guide will describe proven novel approaches related to two critical steps in the Iowa EBP model highlighted in orange, with examples in the context of decreasing central line associated bloodstream infections. (See Figure 3)

1. Pilot the Change in practice

2. Institute the Change in Practice.

Figure 3	Pilot the Change in Practice	
	Iowa Model	**Novel Approach**
1	Select outcomes to be achieved	1.a. Select one key performance indicator (KPI) that is validated and reliably collected at the organization
		1.b. Identify the evidence-based practice that can be easily observed and is critical to the desired KPI achievement
2	Collect baseline data	2.a. Obtain KPI baseline data and create a statistical control chart
		2.b. Conduct baseline observations to understand the current state of the practice in question
3	Design evidence-based practice (EBP) guideline(s)	3.a. Design DRAFT EBP guidelines and create a detailed process map reflecting the ideal the new practice
		3.b Educate using Just in Time (JIT) technique a one page "how to" guide
		3.c. Educate using a short video, no more than 3 – 4 minutes, using frontline associates on the pilot unit to demonstrate the new practice
4	Implement EBP on pilot units	4.a. Pilot new practice on a single unit starting with a single patient, utilizing robust PDSA cycles; gradually increase the observations to additional patients
		4.b. Gradually spread pilot across the pilot unit, incrementally increasing # of PDSA cycles until entire unit is included
		4.c. Obtain feedback regarding barriers and/or burden in the new practice
		4.d. Adjust new practice based upon associate feedback with each PDSA cycle. Edit observation check sheet and process map to reflect improvement iterations
5	Evaluate the process and outcomes	5.a. Aggregate and analyze observation data and compare to baseline.

		5.b. Update control chart
6	Modify the practice guidelines	6.a. Update guidelines after at least 30 PDSA cycles have been conducted and evaluated
		6.b. Update detailed process map after at least 30 PDSA cycles have been conducted, evaluated and improvements implemented
		6.c. Have early wins been achieved in KPI and the process indicator so that the practice can be tested further?

Each novel approach will be described in detail in the pages to follow.

Pilot the Change in Practice:

Step 1

	Iowa Model	**Novel Approach**	Example
1	Select outcomes to be achieved	1.a. Select one **key performance indicator** (KPI) that is validated and reliably collected at the organization	• CLABSI SIR • Source: NHSN TAP Report
		1.b. Identify the **evidence-based practice** that can be easily observed and is critical to the desired KPI achievement	• Central line dressing change

1.a. Select a key performance indicator: Explore external databases to identify a KPI that is collected, validated, and of strategic importance to your organization:

➢ Selected External Data Bases [5]

- Leapfrog
- National Database of Nursing Quality Indicators (NDNQI)
- National Healthcare Safety Network (NHSN)
    - Targeted Assessment for Prevention (TAP) Report
- Centers for Medicare & Medicaid Services (CMS)
    - Dartmouth Atlas Project (DAP)
- Healthcare Effectiveness Data and Information Set (HEDIS)
- Hospital Consumer Assessment of Healthcare Providers and Systems (HCAHPS)
- National Hospital Ambulatory Medical Care Survey (NHAMCS)
- National Surgical Quality Improvement Program (NSQIP)
- Outcome and Assessment Information Set (OASIS)
- Pediatric Quality Measures Program (PQMP)
- Prescription Drug Monitoring Programs (PDMPs)
- Society for Thoracic Surgeons General Thoracic Surgery Database (STS GTSD)
- United States Health Information Knowledgebase (USHIK) and Meaningful Use (MU)

Many of these data found in the external databases lag behind current state by several weeks or months, which is a challenge. Most healthcare organizations are collecting these data in real-time to enable outcome monitoring during the pilot and implementation of EBP.

1.b. Identify the evidence-based practice and build a process map:

- Build a detailed process map with the team.
    - Based upon your detailed process map (see Figure 4), collaboratively identify and prioritize the most critical step in the process that is key to the successful outcome of the process and is easily observed.
    - Develop an observation check sheet and record whether the step was performed as desired, yes or no. (see Figure 5)

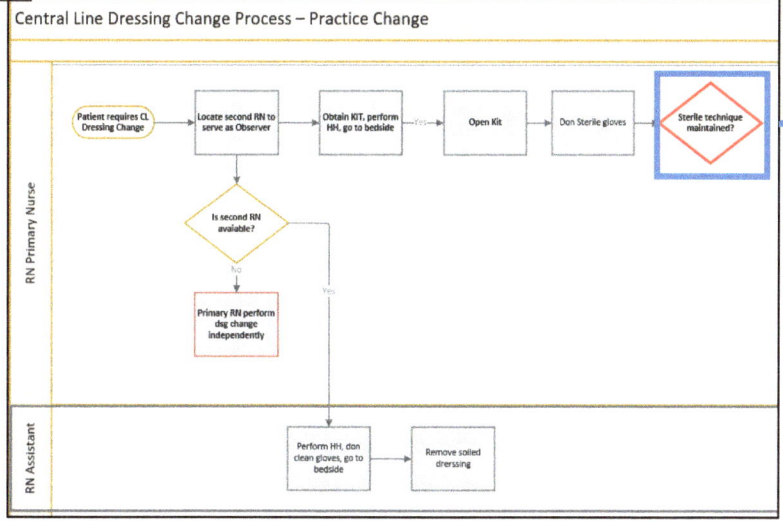

Figure 4

Figure 5

Pilot the Change in Practice:

Step 2

	Iowa Model	Novel Approach	Example
2	Collect baseline data	2.a. Collect KPI baseline data and create a statistical control chart	• CLABSI SIR • Source: NHSN TAP Report
		2.b. Conduct baseline observations to understand the current state of the practice in question	• Observe central line dressing change

2.a. Obtain key performance indicator baseline data and create a statistical control chart: If you do not have access to statistical software, you can create a control chart in Excel. See the *link* below for a step-by-step tutorial. Note: It is recommended you have at least 30 data points to create a valid control chart. If this is not possible, collect as much historical data as you can. You may consider creating a time series plot as an alternative if building a control chart is not possible.

> *Link:* https://www.extendoffice.com/documents/excel/2429-excel-control-chart.html

Control charts are also known as Shewhart charts, named after their inventor, Walter Shewhart of Bell Labs. There are many different types of control charts that can be used depending on the type of process data. In my experience, the two most useful control charts in healthcare are the Individuals Chart (I Chart) and the Proportion Chart (P Chart). This guide will describe the characteristics and rules related to the I and P charts.

Why a control chart?

The control chart offers a clear and concise data visual that tells a story over time. It indicates when the process is in control or out of control. A control chart helps leaders in their understanding and interpretation of when and how to react to variation. It enables leaders and others to identify the presence of unusual circumstances reflected in the data that require further investigation. [9]

What are the elements of a control chart?

The control chart (see Figure 6) is a graph used to study how a process changes over time. Data are plotted in time order. A control chart always has a central line for the average or mean, an upper line for the upper control limit (UCL), and a lower control limit (LCL). The control limits are drawn at distances of 3 sigma (3σ) or three standard deviations above and below the mean. The control limits represent the process variation. [8] In healthcare, the calculated LCL can be below zero, which in many cases does not make sense. When this occurs, you can set the LCL to zero.

This versatile data visualization tool is used by a variety of industries and is considered one of the seven basic quality tools. [9]

Points that fall randomly within the control limits indicate that your process is in control and exhibits only common cause or normal variation. Points that fall outside the control limits or display a nonrandom pattern indicate that your process is out of control and that special-cause variation is present. Detailed description to follow.

Figure 6

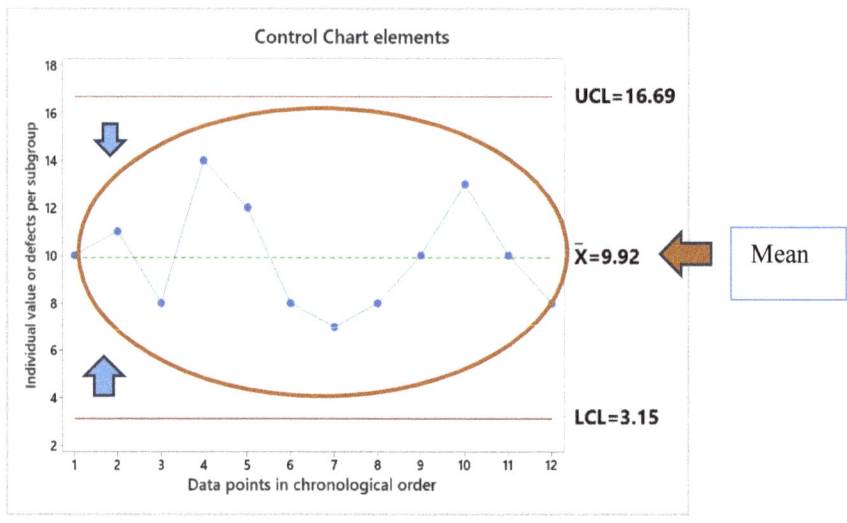

Note: Control limits are not specification limits. Specification limits represent goals based on customer and/or organizational requirements. Spec limits indicate the amount of variation the organization is willing to tolerate in the process. In healthcare, specification limits serve as your goal and can be noted. Baseline data points plotted on a control chart will enable an understanding of performance prior to implementing EBP. The control chart will reflect the magnitude of the problem. Do not confuse the center line with the target value for your process. The target is your desired outcome. The center line is the actual mean performance. [8]

How would a control chart support the assessment of the impact of EBP?

A control chart can be used to assess the outcome or KPI resulting from a new practice. With control charts, it is easy to compare shifts in the process mean and changes in the process variation. Control charts are a reliable way to communicate the performance of your process during a specific time period, for example, before and after the implementation of EBP. [9]

Individual Chart (I Chart)

An I Chart is a control chart used when plotting continuous data. Continuous data is a quantitative or numerical variable that can theoretically take on an infinite number of values based on the accuracy of the instrument and the measuring instrument used. Examples of continuous data include CLABSI standard infection ratio, length of stay, and body temperature. [8]

Proportion Chart (P Chart)

A P Chart is a control chart used when plotting attribute data. Attribute data are data that have a quality characteristic, this is simply a "yes" or a "no" and cannot be divided any further. A P chart monitors the proportion of nonconforming units or defects in a sample. Examples in healthcare include the ratio of the raw # of patient falls as a proportion of the raw number of patient days in a specified period of time. Another example is the ratio of the raw number of CLABSI events as a proportion of the raw number of central line days in a specified period of time.

How is a control chart interpreted?

The tests for special causes assess whether the plotted points are randomly distributed within the control limits. There are four primary tests to use when interpreting an I Chart or a P Chart.

Use the four tests for special causes to determine which observations you may need to investigate and to identify specific patterns and trends in your data. Each of the tests for special causes detects a specific pattern or trend in your data, which reveals a different aspect of process instability. [8]

***Test 1*: One point greater than three standard deviations (3σ) from the center line**

➢ A data point above the UCL or below the LCL. *Test 1* is universally recognized as necessary for the **detection of out-of-control situations**. If small shifts in the process are of interest, you can use *Test*

2 to supplement *Test 1* to create a control chart that has greater sensitivity. [8]

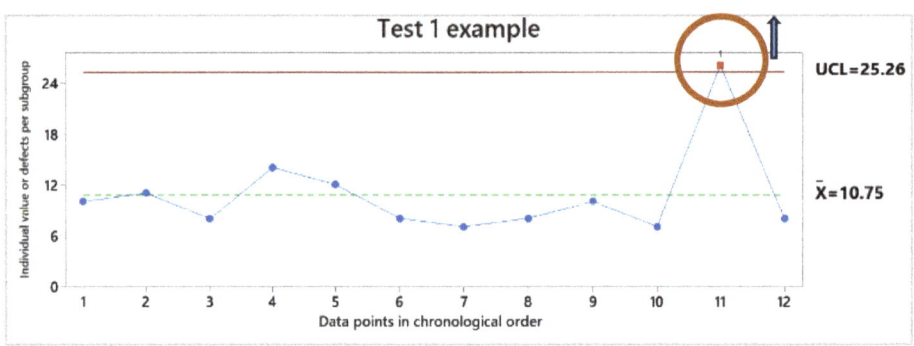

Test 2: Nine points in a row on the same side of the center line

- **Identifies shifts** in the proportion of defectives or values for the process. [8]

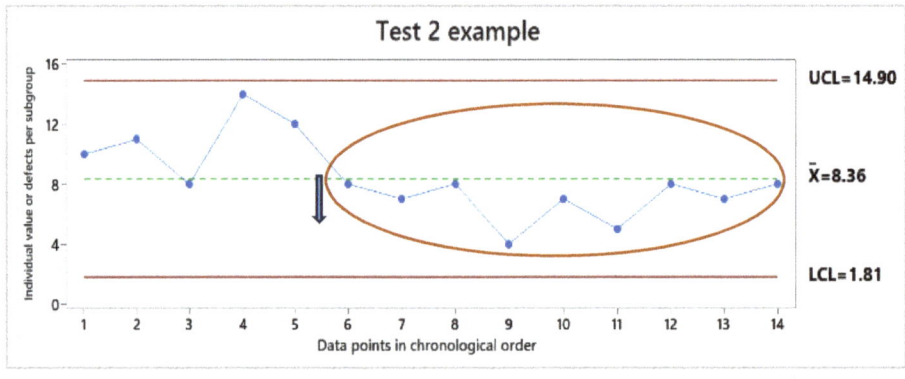

Test 3: **Six points in a row, all increasing or all decreasing**

➢ **Detects trends.** This test looks for a series of six consecutive points that consistently increase in value or decrease in value. [8]

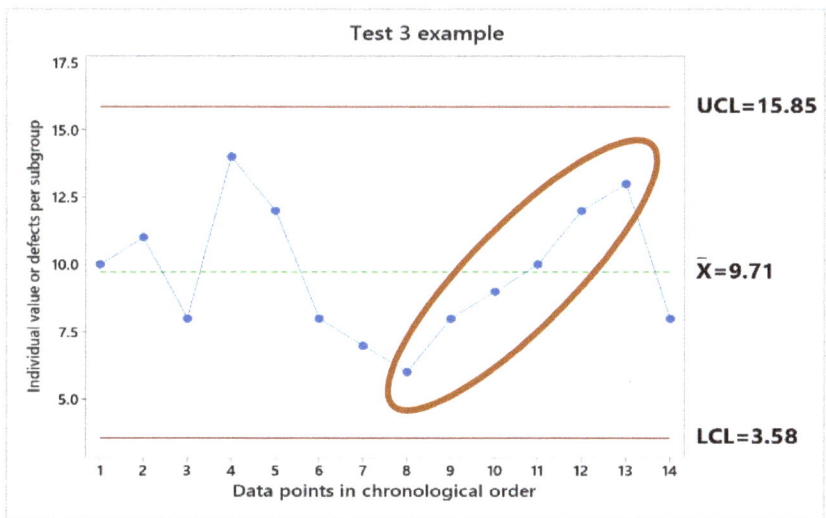

Test 4: **Fourteen points in a row, alternating up and down**

➢ **Detects systematic variation**. You want the pattern of variation in a process to be random, but a point that fails *Test 4* might indicate that the pattern of variation is predictable. [8]

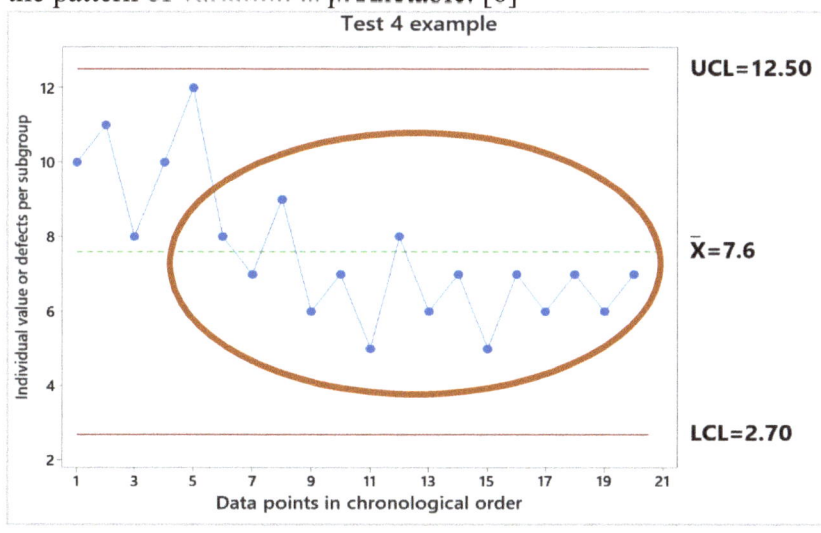

What is the value in creating "stages" to understand the impact EBP had on the KPI?

There is great value in creating a baseline followed by a demarcation to signify when an improvement has been implemented. The challenge is that the data points may occur monthly or quarterly, so it will take time. As John Kotter notes in his work on change management, it is important to celebrate the small wins, understanding that one data point does not make a trend. The team needs to know that there is an encouraging first data point!

Use stages to create a historical control chart that shows how a KPI changes over specific periods of time. You must recalculate the center line and control limits for each stage. This is an example of a historical I Chart that compares baseline and after implementation of EBP. There are two distinct demarcations where the UCL, LCL, and mean are recalculated.[9]

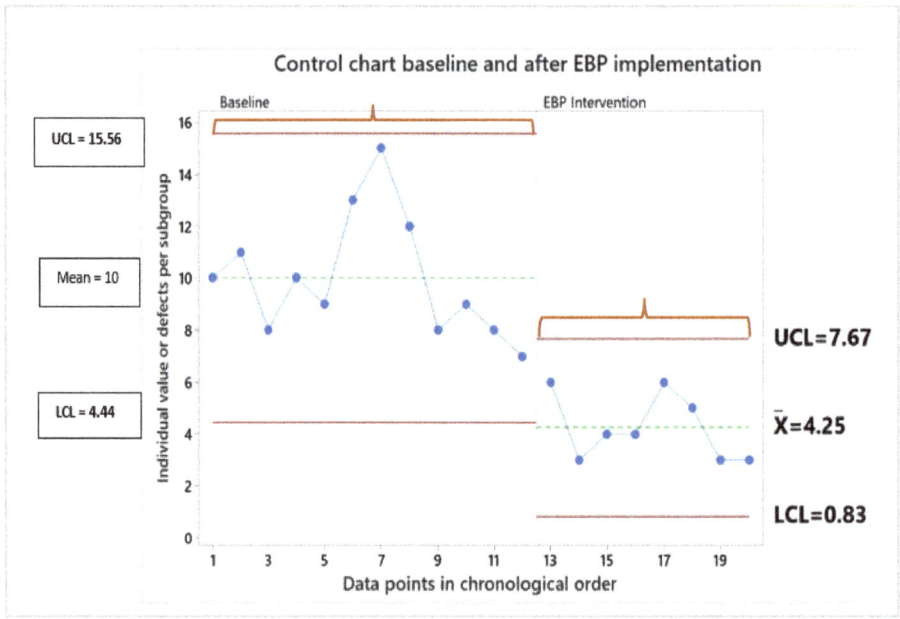

Conclusion: The KPI mean has decreased from 10 to 4.25, and the UCL has decreased from 15.56 to 7.67. After the implementation of EBP, the data points exhibit desirable central tendency. At this juncture, the process is in control and does not trigger tests 1 – 4.

> *Note*: *To take this a step further, perform a 2-sample t-test, along with a P value calculation, to understand whether this represents a statistically significant improvement.*

Congratulate the team and share this information with the pilot unit as the desirable outcomes begin to happen! Celebrate the small wins.

2.b. Conduct baseline observations to understand the current state of the practice in question: It is important to ensure inter and intra-rater reliability. Observations, although challenging, are critical and one of the more difficult activities to accomplish. Competing priorities and lack of ownership are contributing factors to the challenges in performing observations.

> *Note*: *It is important to ensure that observations are conducted with objectivity, in the spirit of curiosity and learning, rather than in a punitive fashion. Bias inherently occurs when associates are aware they are being observed. It is important to ask permission to observe and reassure the associate that the observation is for understanding and not an element of their performance evaluation.*

Inter-rater reliability

Inter-rater reliability refers to the extent to which two or more individuals agree. [6] Suppose two individuals were sent to a nursing unit to observe a central line dressing change, the execution of sterile technique throughout the process, the use of supplies, and the overall appearance of the dressing upon completion. If the observers agreed perfectly on all items, then interrater reliability would be perfect. Interrater reliability is enhanced by training observers, providing them with a guide for recording their observations, monitoring the quality of the data collection over time to see that people are not burning out, and offering a chance to discuss difficult issues or problems. In some circumstances, it is best to have clinical associates observe certain activities such as sterile technique. In other circumstances, it is best to have a variety of observers who see the world differently and may offer unique insights. [6]

Intra-rater reliability

Intra-rater reliability refers to a single individual's consistency of measurement. This can be enhanced by training, monitoring, and continuous education. [6]

Figure 7

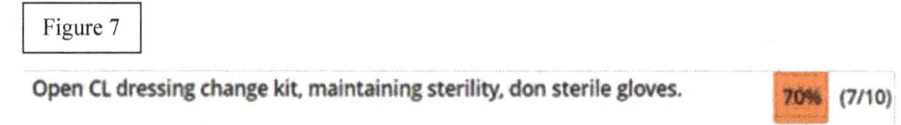

Conclusion: Seven of ten observations (70%) revealed a break in sterile technique.

> *Note: It is important to state this finding in a respectful manner, for example:*
> *"It was observed that 70% of the time, there was an **inadvertent** break in sterile technique."*

Pilot the Change in Practice

Step 3

	Iowa Model	**Novel Approach**	Example
3	Design EBP guidelines	3.a. Design DRAFT EBP guidelines and create a detailed process map reflecting the ideal EBP practice	• Process map reflecting EBP re: Central line dressing change
		3.b. Educate using the Just in Time (JIT) technique, a one-page "how to" guide	• JIT one pager – key elements in Central line dressing change
		3.c. Educate using a short video, no more than 3 – 4 minutes	• Video created with the nursing leader and nurse educator on the pilot unit

3.a. Design Draft EBP guidelines and create a detailed process map reflecting the ideal EBP

The draft guidelines should be just that, a working draft that you expect will need edits after the pilot phase of EBP implementation.

The detailed process map should reflect the ideal EBP practice you are aiming to implement. (see Figure 8) The process map should be collaboratively developed with the team and can be used as a teaching tool. It also serves as a repository of the EBP implementation journey should you need to share it with senior leadership or an accrediting body. It may be useful to number the primary process steps to support data collection when observing. Use standard basic process map symbols when creating a process map. [8] (see Figure 9)

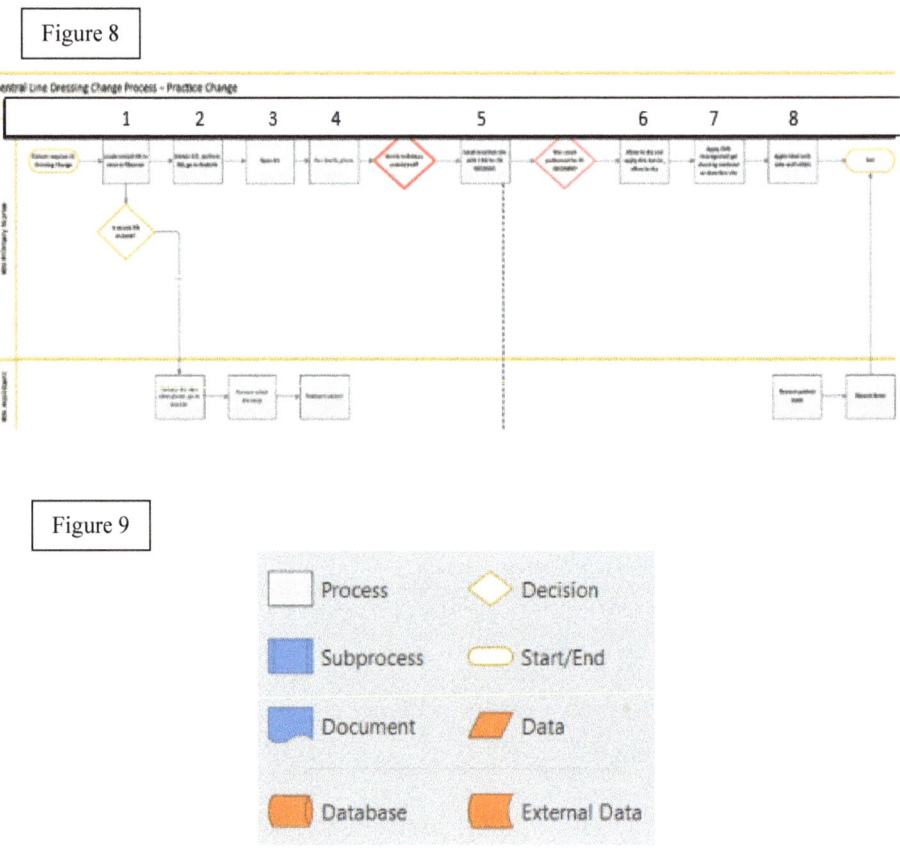

Figure 8

Figure 9

3.c. Educate using the Just in Time (JIT) technique.

- One page "how to" guide

- Short video using frontline associates who work on the pilot unit.

What is Just in Time training, and when is it useful?

Just in Time Training is about presenting short snippets of information in bite-sized chunks when they are needed. Learners can access short, highly relevant content via responsive technology. This is useful as you pilot a new practice without delay. (see Figure 10)

Note: *You do not have to train everyone on the unit, just those associates who will be performing the new practice. Eventually, the training may be more formal as part of annual competencies, but this efficient way to train is helpful when rolling out a pilot. The associate can make instant use of the newly learned information, which is what makes it Just in Time.* [7]

Figure 10

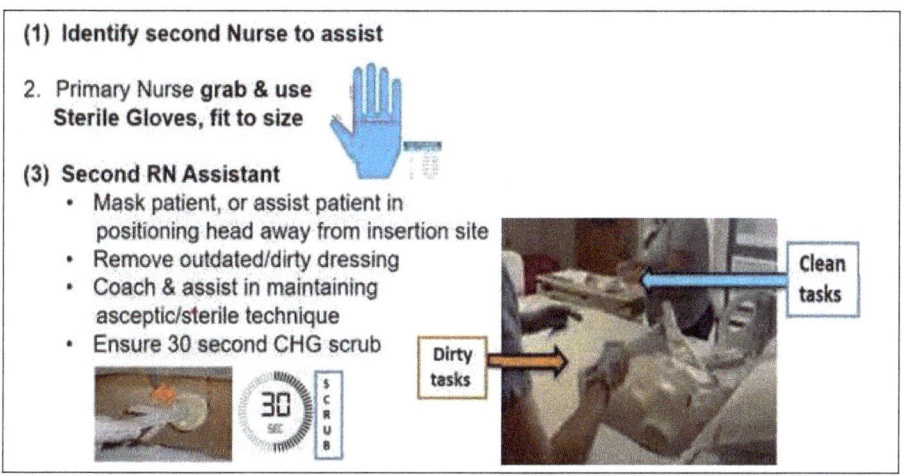

Pilot the Change in Practice

Step 4

	Iowa Model	Novel Approach	Example
4	Implement EBP on pilot units	4.a. Pilot new practice on a single unit starting with a single patient, utilizing robust PDSA cycles; gradually increase the observations to additional patients	• JIT training during the huddle • Assign a responsible person to observe new practice. • Conduct a PDSA cycle with each observation.
		4.b. Gradually spread the pilot across the pilot unit, incrementally increasing # of PDSA cycles until the entire unit is included	• JIT one pager & video – key elements in Central line dressing change
		4.c. Obtain feedback regarding barriers and/or burdens in the new practice	• Observers address barriers and/or burdens and mitigate or eliminate
		4.d. Adjust new process as needed based upon associated feedback with each PDSA cycle	• Observers edit observation check sheet and process map to reflect improvement iterations

What is a PDSA cycle and why is it important?

The Plan-Do-Study-Act (PDSA) cycle is a scientific method to test a change prior to implementation. This is extremely critical to the success of your implementation. In my experience, this has been the primary failure mode that is either omitted or poorly executed due to a lack of rigor involved in executing correctly.

To perform PDSA cycles properly, it is important to go through the prescribed four steps in the thinking process. Plan – Do – Study – Act. It is best to assign a person or small group of people to conduct the PDSA from start to finish, assessing performance of each step in the process and identifying barriers to performance. Once a PDSA cycle is complete, evaluation of the performance, and immediate mitigation or elimination of barriers should occur prior to testing again.

Utilization of the PDSA worksheets is important as you and your teams are learning how to perform and evaluate a change using PDSA cycles. Once you are familiar with the process, it may not be necessary to complete the tool in its entirety. It will always be necessary to note the incremental improvements and then conduct the next PDSA cycle to evaluate the effectiveness of the improvement. [10]

For more information on the PDSA, go to the IHI (Institute for Healthcare Improvement) Web site.

When conducting PDSA cycles, you will need to keep in mind the following:

- **Identify one or more observer**— Perform observations in real-time and records any discrepancies observed in the new practice. Then, obtain feedback and suggestions for improvement from the person performing the new practice and address

- **Maintain defined boundaries**—Each PDSA cycle should have defined boundaries, process steps, and an observation tool so that the observer stays within the scope

- **Keep you sample size small** —PDSAs should incrementally increase as the associates performing the new practice can be trained using JIT techniques. Attempt to collect observation data on a sample, enough to observe 30 times ideally. Once the observations and feedback have been addressed and the process is refined accordingly, the implementation can be broadened to include additional units.

PDSA Planning Worksheet (see Figure 11)

Complete the PDSA planning worksheet with key members of the team prior to beginning your observations.

- ➢ **Overarching Aim**: Write a concise statement of the goal regarding your key performance indicator.
- ➢ **New Practice**: Write a concise summary statement describing the new practice.

PLAN: Complete sections under the Plan category: This is the who, what, where, when, and how. Note: Write a clear and measurable hypothesis statement that will be evaluated with each PDSA.

Figure 11

PDSA Planning Worksheet	
Today's Date: (Date)	Lead: (Name)
Overarching Aim:	Reduce CLABSI SIR from mean of 0.80 to less than 0.589 by (date)
New practice	2 RN central line dressing change separating soiled and sterile tasks
PLAN	
What will you try?	New practice
When?	(date)
Who will be involved?	Lead, observers
Who is observing?	Jane
Team	Nurses on pilot unit
Patients	Patient with central line who is due for dressing change
What is your hypothesis?	When the new practice is performed, there will be zero lapses in sterile technique
What tool will you use to observe?	See observation tool in Small Tests of Change worksheet (interrater reliability confirmed)
Where will you record your evaluation and opportunities to improve?	In real time, on the Small Tests of Change worksheet
Who will update the observation tool if needed?	Observer who has determined a change needs to be made to reduce burden or improve ease for the nurses
Who will communicate with the pilot unit leadership and associates about this plan? When?	Lead

Small Tests of Change Worksheet (see Figure 12)

This is where you document each PDSA cycle.

- ➢ **Do:** It is best to use a standard observation tool in this section. Tally up the results (number of yes and no observations).

- ➢ **Study:** Ask for feedback from those performing the new practice. What were the challenges or barriers to performing the new practice with ease and confidence? Was the hypothesis true? (Circle YES or NO)

➢ **Act:** Based upon your observations and feedback from those performing the new practice, what incremental improvement(s) can be made before the next PDSA to improve the process?

Figure 12

Small Tests of Change			
Today's Date:	Observer:		
Process Measure:	New Practice: 2 RN CL dressing change		
Do			
CENTRAL LINE DRESSING CHANGE Teaching and Observation Tool: REV 1 (09.07.22)	YES	NO	**Study** - # lapses in sterile technique _____ Nurse feedback: - Challenges & suggestions: **Act** - How will you improve the new practice before next PDSA?
1. Gather supplies: STERILE GLOVES, FIT TO SIZE Central Line dressing kit, don non-sterile gloves, mask			
Comments			
2. ASSISTANT and PRIMARY Nurses Perform hand hygiene, don nonsterile gloves and mask			
Comments			
3. ASSISTANT HELPS PATIENT cover nose and mouth with MASK			
Comments:			
4. ASSISTANT Remove Dirty Dressing			
Comments:			
5. ASSISTANT REMOVE DIRTY GLOVES & Perform hand hygiene, don CLEAN PAIR non-sterile gloves			
Comments:			
6. PRIMARY NURSE Open CL dressing change KIT, maintain sterility, don STERILE GLOVES, FIT TO SIZE			
Comments:			
7. PRIMARY NURSE activate CHG applicator & thoroughly cleans insertion site for 30 SECONDS			
Comments:			
8. PRIMARY NURSE apply skin prep to area under dressing and catheter stabilization device, and allow to dry			
Comments:			
9. PRIMARY NURSE apply CHG impregnated gel dressing centered over insertion site			
Comments:			
10. PRIMARY NURSE apply catheter stabilization device if being used			
Comments:			
11. If Bio patch is applied, blue side is up and centered around lumen between catheter and skin			
Comments: *If NA, leave answer BLANK*			
12. PRIMARY NURSE label dressing with date and initials, and adhere to dressing			
Comments:			
13. ASSISTANT help pt remove mask, discard items, remove gloves and perform hand hygiene on way out door			
Comments:			
Hypothesis: When the new CL dressing change practice is performed, there will be zero lapses in sterile technique. YES NO			

Below is an example of a PDSA rollout plan. (see Figure 13) It is imperative to develop your plan to carry out small tests of change, aka PDSAs, without delay. Gradually increase and continue to observe and address barriers and issues in real-time. It is ideal if the observer is familiar with the PDSA model and iterative process.

Figure 13

Pilot Unit	PDSAs	Associate to observe	Observer	Sterile Technique Process Indicator	
C22				# Lapses	Process step where lapse occurred & solution
Day 1	Pt BN	Nurse	Jane	1	Step 4: The nurse touched the mask; solution: position assistant near HOB
Day 2	Pt SC	Nurse	Jane		
	Pt GW	Nurse	Tennille		
Day 3	Pt TS	Nurse	Tennille		
	Pt MC	Nurse	Rachael		
	Pt HH	Nurse	Rachael		
Day 4	Pt WH	Nurse	Jane		
↓	Pt FS	Nurse	Jane		
	Pt RH	Nurse	Jane		
	Pt CC	Nurse	Jane		

Continue PDSAs each day; after 30 improvement iterations, the process should be ready to spread.

Pilot the Change in Practice

Step 5

	Iowa Model	**Novel Approach**	Example
5	Evaluate the process and outcomes	5.a. Aggregate and analyze observation data and compare it to baseline.	• Determine the percentage of time your hypothesis was proved to be true.
		5.b. Update control chart in stages	• Demarcate the control chart once EBP has been implemented

5.a. Aggregate and analyze observation data and compare it to baseline. Note the percentage of time your hypothesis proved to be true.

| Open CL dressing change kit, maintaining sterility, don sterile gloves. | 100% | (2/2) |

Conclusion: When the EBP practice for central line dressing change is performed, separating soiled and sterile tasks, sterility is maintained 100% of the time. The hypothesis was proven true 100% of the time.

> *Note: During the pilot and adoption phases, additional observations are required until the practice is consistently performed as it was designed.*

5.b. Update baseline KPI control chart: Once the pilot has spread to the entire unit, update the unit specific control chart. It may also be an interesting exercise to update the organizational control chart as well.

> *Note: The observation data is available and is an indication that the new practice is performed as designed. Since you are expecting a positive impact on your KPI because of the implementation of*

EBP, tracking both compliance with the new practice and the KPI will be important.

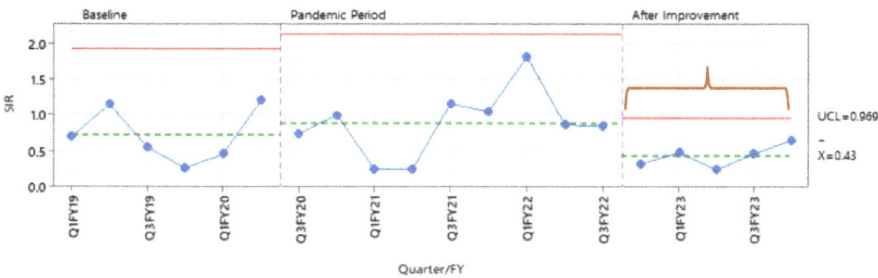

Conclusion: After improvement through EBP, we can state that the process is in control. The quarterly variation demonstrates a strong central tendency around the mean. The mean CLABSI SIR is 0.43 as of Q4FY23. Congratulate the team!

Recommendation: Continue to periodically observe the new EBP to ensure unwarranted variation is not occurring.

So, when is it time to declare a win? When do we have enough data to influence others?

These are important considerations. When you have had success on a single pilot unit, it is important to document your PDSA methodology and results with data visuals that are easily understood by all. The data visuals you decide to use will depend on your audience. Select the most convincing and understandable data visual that will influence your audience.

	Institute the Change in Practice	
	Iowa Model	**Novel Approach**
1	Monitor and analyze structure, process, and outcome data	1.a. Select an appropriate governance structure to assess for effectiveness
		1.b. Continue to observe the new EBP by selecting a small sample across multiple units to ensure the practice is performed as designed and educated.
		1.c. Continue to update the control chart with the KPI data. React accordingly to special causes and tests 1,2,3 4

Prepare an update to the organization to share the results and include testimonials from the associates who perform the new practice. Communicate and present to key stakeholders, including governing committees and councils.

I have found that making space for the leaders to decide what they would like to pilot and implement in their unit is the best way to spread. Positive momentum usually happens when the story is clear and compelling.

> *Note: Be sure you have a short presentation that is pertinent to your audience so that your message is compelling and not lost in the minutia.*

	Iowa Model	Novel Approach	Example
1	Monitor and analyze structure, process, and outcome data	1.a. Select an appropriate governance structure to assess for effectiveness	• Observe CLABSI Council event review debriefs and lessons learned. • Continually improve through regular critiques and feedback.
		1.b. Continue to observe the new EBP by selecting a small sample across multiple units to ensure the practice is performed as designed and educated.	• Set up an observation calendar. • Attempt to observe two central line dressing changes per month on each unit. • Coach to standard and continue to identify any barriers to performance and mitigate
		1.c. Continue to update the control chart with the KPI data. React accordingly to special cause and tests 1,2,3 4	• Update control chart and coach others about how to interpret the findings

Governance Structure:

Most organizations have a team that pays special attention to strategic outcomes in your organization. Ensure this team is multidisciplinary, including physicians and makes data-driven decisions. Consider the use of a standardized repository for events in question. Aggregate and communicate lessons learned.

Scale across the organization:

As you spread to additional units and implement the new practice across the organization, it will still be important to be sensitive to the differences between units or care settings.

PDSAs are still of value and should be conducted. However, it is likely this phase will have a shorter timeline, depending on the nuances and differences on the unit. You may be able to spread to additional units in pairs instead of one by one to escalate the spread more quickly.

When PDSAs are conducted well, the initial pilot unit should have smoothed and refined the process enough to spread with little to no additional improvements needed.

Update control chart

Continue to monitor the key process indicator and set up a schedule to randomly observe the new performance to verify it is being performed to standard.

Track your business case

Several examples to think about when considering your business case include but are not limited to:

> ➢ Reduction in additional cost of care
>> o Additional length of stay, medications, higher level of care

- Favorable pay for performance reimbursement from CMS
    - Quality Based Reimbursement (Maryland)
    - Value-Based Purchasing
- Favorable community reputation
- Reduction in patient harm

In closing, I would like to wish you all the best on your journey. With rigor and attention up front, you can and will be successful and reap the rewards of implementing evidenced-based practice.

Please contact me if you are interested in one-on-one coaching.

Author contact information: Shirleycahillimages@gmail.com

References

1. https://canberra.libguides.com/evidence

2. https://www.ncbi.nlm.nih.gov/books/NBK589676/#:~:text=The%20ACE%20Star%20model%20is,and%20process%20and%20outcome%20evaluation. Different models

3. Roe-Prior P. Evidence-Based Practice. 2022 May-Jun 01J Nurses Prof Dev. 38(3):177-178. [PubMed]

4. Shirey MR, Hauck SL, Embree JL, Kinner TJ, Schaar GL, Phillips LA, Ashby SR, Swenty CF, McCool IA. Showcasing differences between quality improvement, evidence-based practice, and research. J Contin Educ Nurs. 2011 Feb;42(2):57-68; quiz 69-70. [PubMed]

5. https://pubmed.ncbi.nlm.nih.gov/7579545

6. https://www.sciencedirect.com/topics/nursing-and-health-professions/interrater-reliability

7. https://myelearningworld.com/what-is-just-in-time-learning/

8. Understanding control charts - Minitab

9. https://asq.org/quality-resources/control-chart#:~:text=The%20control%20chart%20is%20a,for%20the%20lower%20control%20limit.

10. Plan-Do-Study-Act (PDSA) Directions and Examples | Agency for Healthcare Research and Quality (ahrq.gov)

Appendix
PDSA Planning Worksheet

PDSA Planning Worksheet	
Today's Date:	Lead:
Overarching Aim:	
Process Measure:	
PLAN	
What will you try?	
When?	
Who will be involved?	
Who is observing?	
Team	
Patients	
What is your hypothesis?	
What tool will you use to observe?	
How will you record your evaluation and opportunities to improve?	
Who will update the observation tool if needed?	
Who will communicate with the pilot unit leadership and associates about this plan? When?	

Small Tests of Change Worksheet

Today's Date:	Observer:	
Process Measure:	New Practice:	
Do		
Insert Data Collection tool		**Study** - # errors Feedback from those performing the new practice - Challenges & suggestions: **Act** - How will you improve the new practice before next PDSA?
Hypothesis True?	YES	NO

www.ingramcontent.com/pod-product-compliance
Lightning Source LLC
LaVergne TN
LVHW072123060526
838201LV00068B/4956